yukibooks.com/b/8a68d6

bébé

baby

garçon

boy

amis

friends

fille

girl

sourire

smile

pleurer

cry

cheveux

hair

oeil

eye

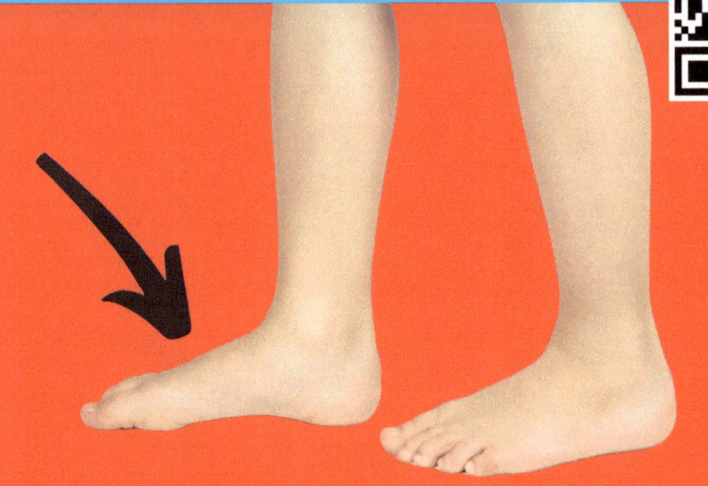

pied

foot

main

hand

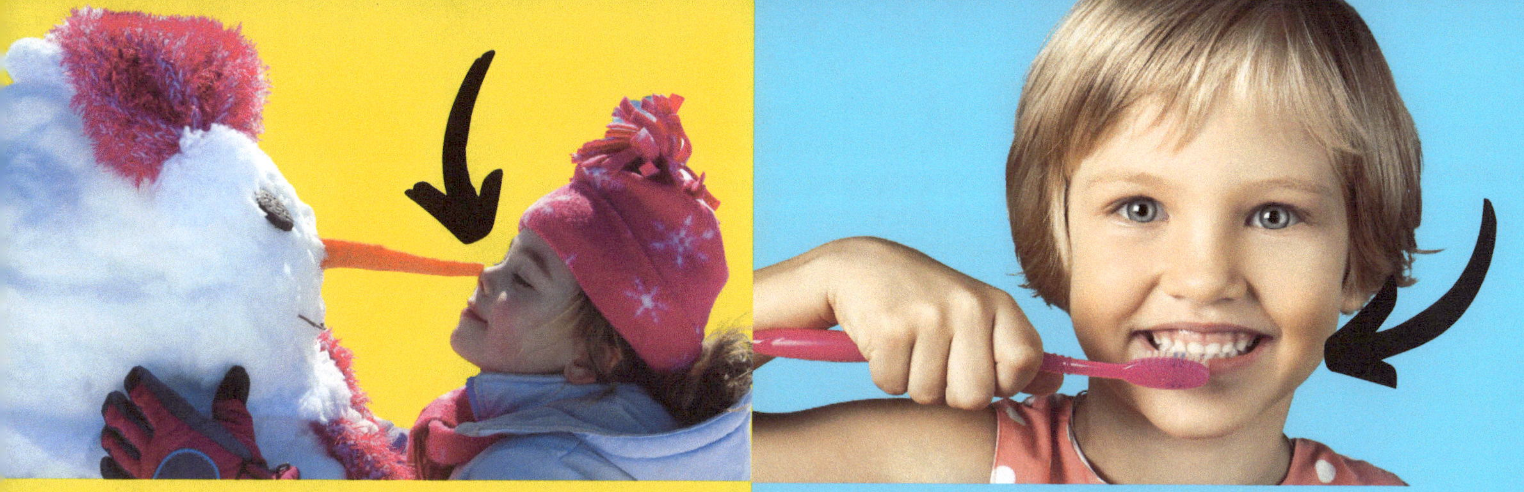

nez

nose

dents

teeth

oreille

ear

langue

tongue

soleil
sun
lune
moon
étoile
star

arbre
tree

oiseau
bird

manteau

coat

pantalon

pants

robe

dress

chaussures

shoes

rouge

red

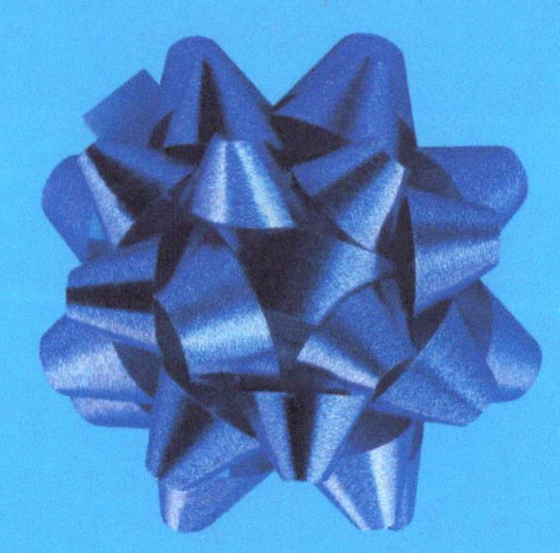

bleu

blue

jaune

yellow

rose

pink

blanc
white
vert
green
noir
black

multicolore
multicolored

arc en ciel

rainbow

pomme
apple

banane
banana

tomate
tomato

orange
orange

carotte

carrot

pois

peas

pomme de terre

potato

maïs

corn

maize

citron

lemon

raisins

grapes

poire

pear

pastèque

watermelon

courgette

🇺🇸 zucchini
🇬🇧 courgette

oeuf

egg

champignon

mushroom

carré

square

rond

circle

rectangle

rectangle

triangle

triangle

chat
cat

chien
dog

poisson

fish

vache

cow

canard

duck

poussin

chick

poule

hen

grenouille

frog

cochon

pig

lapin

rabbit

souris

mouse

cheval

horse

mouton

sheep

fleur

flower

papillon

butterfly

coccinelle
🇺🇸 ladybug
🇬🇧 ladybird

escargot

snail

gâteau

cake

pain

bread

horloge

clock

clé

key

livre

book

ballon

ball

table

table

assiette

plate

chaise

chair

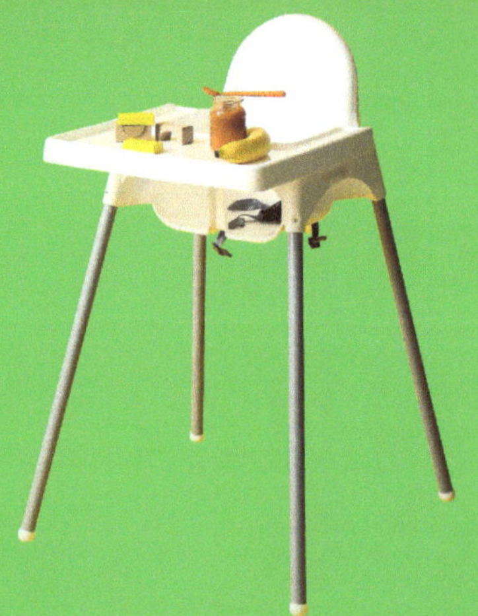

chaise haute

high chair

fourchette

fork

couteau

knife

cuillère

spoon

tasse

cup

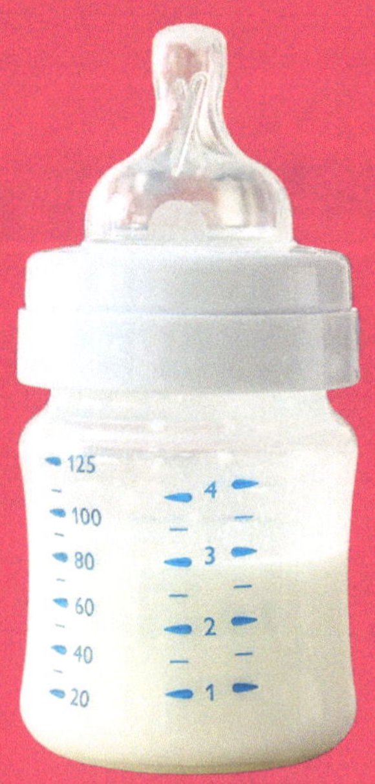

biberon
baby bottle

verre
glass

lit
bed

lit bébé
🇺🇸 crib
🇬🇧 cot

ours en peluche
teddy bear

tétine
🇺🇸 pacifier
🇬🇧 dummy

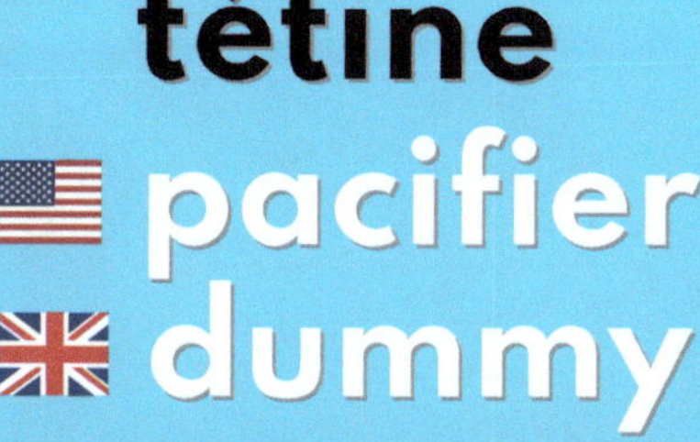

serviette

towel

lavabo

sink

brosse à dents

toothbrush

savon

soap

toilettes
toilets

pot
potty

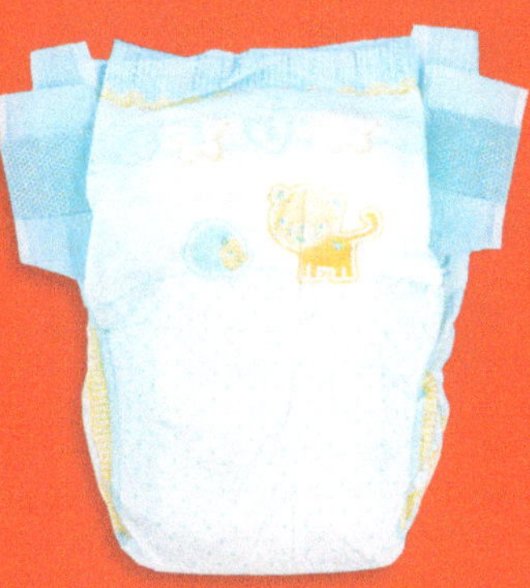

couche
diaper

voiture

car

vélo

bike

avion

plane

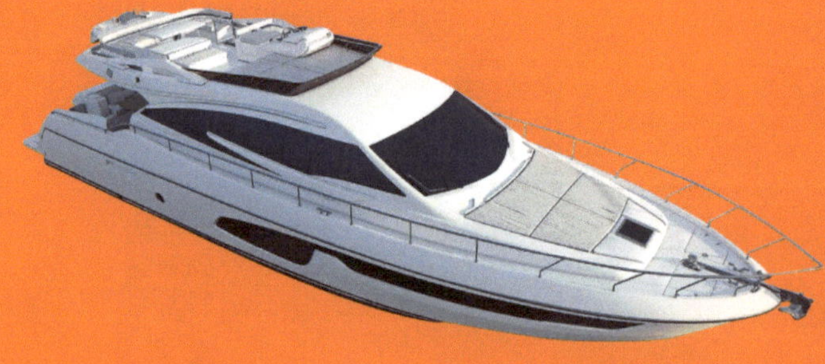

bateau

boat

camion de pompier

firetruck

train

train

jouets

toys

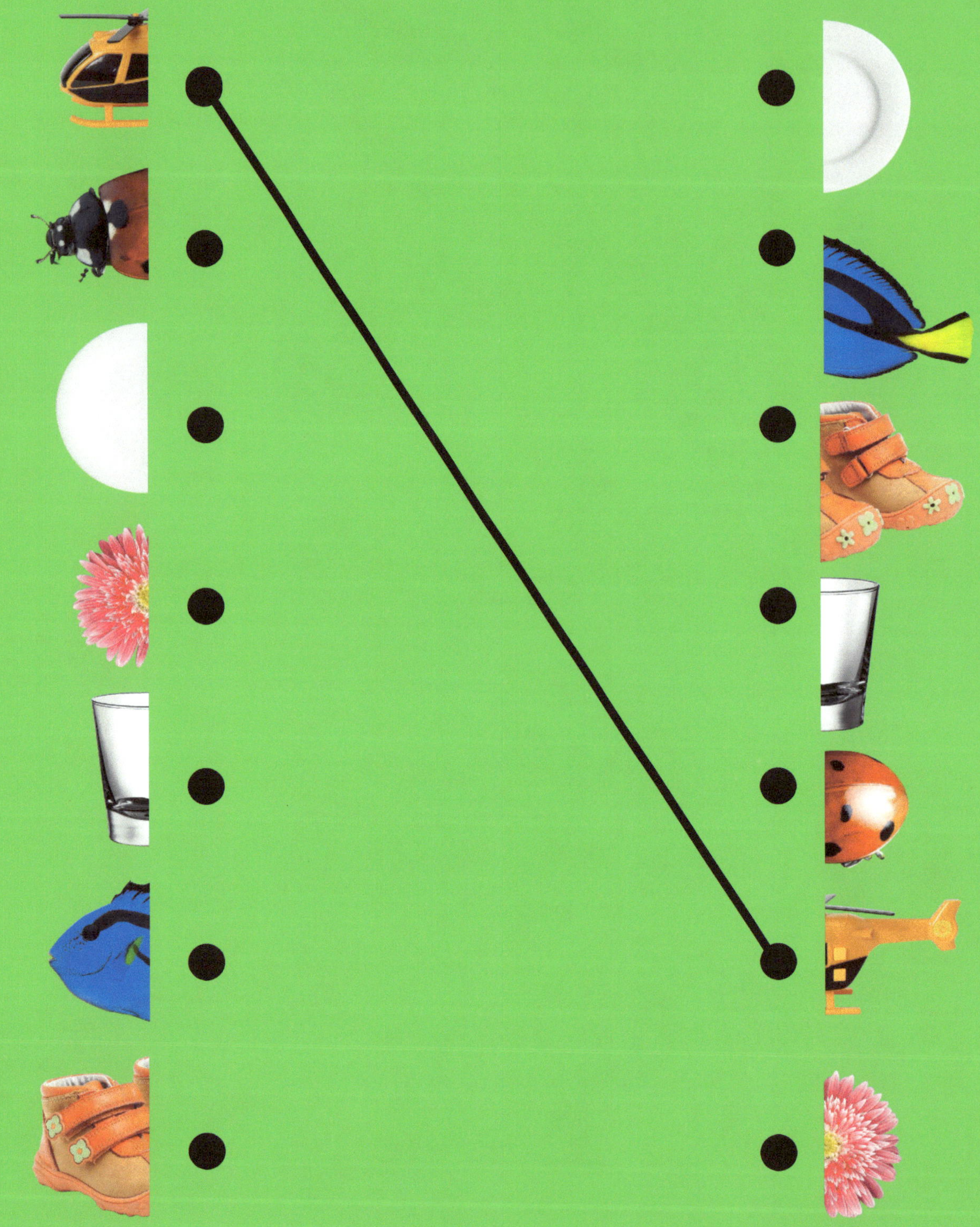

www.ingramcontent.com/pod-product-compliance
Lightning Source LLC
LaVergne TN
LVHW071647180726
843512LV00002B/399